MW00942668

Understanding the Islamic Worldview

By Russ Rodgers

The Generalship of Muhammad
The Rise and Decline of Mobility Doctrine
Fundamentals of Islamic Asymmetric Warfare
Historic Photos of General George Patton

Understanding the Islamic Worldview

by

Russ Rodgers

Cover illustration: a Burger King restaurant in
Riyadh, Saudi Arabia. Photo by Russ Rodgers

ISBN-13: 978-1516880201
ISBN-10: 151688020X

To Chaplain (COL) Michael T. Klein, for enduring mind-numbing days and nights in the field with me... and the chance to hike the hills of Germany together...

...and to Chaplain (LTC) James Boulware, for giving me the encouragement to write this book.

Contents

Introduction

When studying Islam, one can find the essential concepts easily online. There are a plethora of sources available for the eager student to learn the basics and even some advanced topics regarding Islam. There are also plenty of readily available books to do the same. However, I have decided to focus on the worldview of Islam, looking more closely at how that worldview is developed and formed, and how it shapes the decision making process of a Muslim. The reason this is important is because far too many Western analysts of Islam have either accepted a rosy interpretation of the movement, largely fueled by starry-eyed Orientalists from Europe, especially Great Britain, or have attempted to superimpose Western notions of morality on Islam and thus disregard important aspects they wish to ignore.

In addition, there are many who have accepted the idea that Islam is illogical, and that authentic Islam, the revival of which we are witnessing today, is even worse than illogical.[1] Again, nothing could be further from the truth, and is largely driven by once again templating Western ideals onto it. Those who claim that Islam is illogical are starting from the wrong premises driven by a different agenda, either unconsciously or knowingly. Rather, Islam is very logical, as is the revival of authentic Islam. It is completely logical within the bounds of its premises as formulated in the body of early Islamic writings, such as the Qur'an and *hadith* literature.

In the following pages I will provide a look into some essentials of the Islamic worldview. These points are not readily found for the average person in the West, and oftentimes some of them are not well understood even by Muslims. Nevertheless, it is important to understand these principles of the

---

[1] Lee Harris, *The Suicide of Reason: Radical Islam's Threat to the West,* pp 205-213; Robert R. Reilly, *The Closing of the Muslim Mind: How Intellectual Suicide Created the Modern Islamist Crisis,* pp 1-39. The problem here lies mainly in the their conception that "reason" means man determining right and wrong without any revelation outside of mankind, essentially similar to what Immanuel Kant argued in his famous essay "Was ist Aufklärung" in 1784.

Islamic worldview so one can make accurate assessments of what practitioners of the movement do and why they do it. I will readily admit that this small contribution is a compromise, for there are some issues and ideas that require more explanation or inclusion. However, that would require a much larger and more involved text, and the purpose of my work here is to provide you, the reader with a ready tool to help understand how an authentic Muslim thinks and views the world around him.

I should also note that I have used a number of Arabic terms in the text. The purpose here is not to confuse the reader, but to partly familiarize laymen with these terms. A full glossary of italicized words appears as an appendix.

Lastly, I would like to thank those who read the text and provided comments and suggestions for improvement. Their advice was invaluable. Nevertheless, any errors or omissions in the text are my own.

Chapter 1

Some Definitions

Before anything else, we must look at a few definitions so that the meaning of various concepts is clear. When I speak of Islam and Muslims, I am talking about authentic Islam. Authentic Islam is that which is practiced in accordance with the teachings and lifestyle of the last Prophet of *Allah*, Muhammad. While there may be other religions in the world in which a person interested in them may be able to practice many aspects of that religion as they see fit, Islam is one that opposes such an approach. In Islam, one is first and foremost guided by the recitations of Muhammad as the spoken words of *Allah* to the people of the world. Next, they are guided by the actions of Muhammad, or the *sunnah*. Not all actions of the Prophet are considered *sunnah* in the sense that one must imitate them. Some actions are only suggested, while some are forbidden to other Muslims. For example, Muhammad was provided, in Surah 37, an exception to the limit of four wives, being allowed to marry as many women as he desired. Other Muslims are not allowed this dispensation.

So what is the difference between authentic Islam and other versions? When I say this, I'm not speaking of the difference between various Islamic sects, such as Sunnis or Shi'ites. Both of these groups could still be practicing authentic Islam on the basis of following the Qur'an and their *hadith* collections.[2] Instead, I'm referring to the difference between true Islam and what can best be described as "folk Islam."[3] Folk Islam, like any other folk religion, is where only bits and pieces of true Islam are practiced while mixed with various aspects of other religions and philosophies, also known as syncretism. In contrast, authentic Islam is the practice of Islam as the Prophet Muhammad determined through his word and deed. This does not mean that Muslims don't have some latitude, but it does mean that their belief and practice should not contradict instructions and admonitions within the body of early Islamic writings and what was communicated by the Prophet Muhammad. Indeed, it is the place of Muhammad

---

[2] There are essentially two major collections of *hadith* literature, one accepted by Sunnis and the other by Shi'ites.

[3] One can find a good discussion of "folk religion" in Paul G. Hiebert, R. Daniel Shaw, and Tite Tiénou, *Understanding Folk Religion.*

that determines first and foremost if a person is an authentic Muslim. If a person believes that they can follow later people who claim to be prophets, they are denying Muhammad's one admonition that he is the last Prophet of *Allah*. There can be none after him.

The reason true practice is so critical in Islam is that a Muslim's very destiny is driven by the practice of their Islamic *din*, or religion. The Arabic term "*din*" is a difficult one to properly translate. While often rendered in English as "religion," the term more accurately refers to a contract of indebtedness.[4] Thus, when one declares themselves to be a Muslim, they have made a contract with *Allah*, a contract that offers certain blessings and rewards based on the practice of the believer. I will shortly explore this issue of contract more fully.

Discussing such definitions is important, because as I speak of "Islam" or "Muslims," I'm referring to authentic Islam and not to some form of folk Islam. In the eyes of the Prophet Muhammad such folk Islam would by and large not be considered authentic Islam.

---

[4] Edward W. Lane, *An Arabic-English Lexicon in Eight Parts*, Part 3, p. 942.

Chapter 2

The Basis of Practice

What is the basis for the practice of Islam? First and foremost, there is the Qur'an, the recitation of the words of *Allah* from Muhammad. However, the Qur'an, originally written in a form of ancient Arabic, or Mudar is difficult for even modern Arabic readers to use.[5] Therefore, those who work with the Qur'an rely upon *tafsirs*, or commentaries to explain what many passages mean. One does not approach the Qur'an like they do other religious books, such as the Bible. You simply do not open it up to the first chapter and read words like "in the beginning...," nor is the Qur'an organized chronologically. Instead, it is largely organized, with the notable exception of the first chapter, or *surah*, by the size of the chapter, with the largest ones appearing first. More than reading it one should chant or recite the Qur'an, repeating phrases continuously. Such rhythmic chanting allows

---

[5] This was not always the case, as in medieval Islam. See Ibn Khaldûn, *al-Muqaddimah,* Vol. 3, pp 344-353.

for easier memorization of the passages, and one who memorizes the Qur'an gains the title of *hafiz*.

While the Qur'an is explained by *tafsirs*, the source material for the *tafsirs* comes from the *hadith* literature. The *hadith* literature is a convenient term I use to refer to three sets of writings: the *hadith*, or sayings of Muhammad, the *sunnah*, or deeds of Muhammad, and the *sirah*, or historical writings of early Islam. The latter can be similar to the first two, but often contains material dealing with Muhammad's closest companions, or *Salafi*, that may not be readily found in the major *hadith* collections. There is a pretty complex process as to how *hadith* were compiled and classified, and I will not get into that here.[6] Suffice it to say that we should understand a Muslim will look to the *hadith* literature to tell them how to live and act, especially in areas were the Qur'an seems confusing, incomplete, or even silent.

Beyond the *hadith* literature there are two other collections of sources that form and inform the Muslim's life. These are the sayings and rulings of the leaders of what are now called the *madhhabs*, or schools of law. After that, come the rulings of lesser

[6] For details on how the *hadith* is organized and classified, see Ibn al-Salah al-Shahrazuri, *Kitab Ma`rifat anwa` ilm al-hadith* (as *An Introduction to the Science of the Hadith)*.

qadis, or jurists over the centuries, a process referred to as *fiqh*. There are essentially four major *madhhabs* in Sunni Islam (Maliki, Shafa`i, Hanbali, Hanafi), and two within Shi'ite Islam (Ja`fari and Zaidi). There are several other schools for smaller sects, but this need not concern us here. What we need to know is that after the Qur'an and *hadith* literature, a Muslim looks to a particular *madhhab* to explain how to live. Connected here is the need to seek the advice and rulings of *qadis* to explain how *shari`ah*, or Islamic law should be lived out.

Chapter 3

Doing is Worship

The key point to understand here is that authentic Islam is not about belief or mental assent. It's about action, and these actions cover a vast field of one's life, from one's personal conduct to rules about political government. One must DO Islam to be a true Muslim, and that means doing Islam in all of its facets.[7] One cannot simply say "I believe" and that be enough. Again, there is some leeway here, in that *madhhabs* will at times disagree as to how one should live in certain circumstances. For example, regarding warfare, some *madhhabs* say that while engaged in battle it is wrong to knowingly inflict collateral damage on Muslims while attacking non-Muslim forces. However, other jurists disagree and believe that doing so is legitimate so long as the Muslims were not purposely targeted.[8] Therefore, there will be

---

[7] *Tafsir Ibn Kathir*, Vol. 1, pp 110-113.

[8] Al-Tabari, Abu Ja'far Muhammad bin Jarir. *Kitab al-Jihad,* Section 2.

areas where Muslims disagree about certain actions. However, it is very important to note that there is much on which they do agree.

Regarding this issue of action in Islam, it must also be understood that such action is a form of worship. Indeed, worship within Islam goes far beyond the five daily prayers and offering up supplications to *Allah*. One's other actions constitute a form of worship, and thus one's worship life is inextricably intertwined with the rest of one's life. Everything that a Muslim does, so long as it correlates to *shari'ah* and its rulings, is a worshipful act. Concurrently, doing things contrary to *shari'ah* is a form of rebellion, or sinful act. Engaging in evil deeds has its own interesting consequences in Islam as we shall soon see.

It is important here to explain that when I mean "action," I'm not just including physical acts. Islam does allow one to act in the heart, especially if it is too dangerous to speak out (an act of the tongue) or to physically do something (an act of the hand).[9] However, merely believing something is insufficient

---

[9] *Sahih Muslim*, Vol. I, Chap 20, #49; Majid Khadduri. *War and Peace in the Law of Islam,* pp 56-57; Muhammad Ali al-Hashimi. *The Ideal Muslim Society,* pp 108-110.

in Islam. One must show their *iman*, or faith by acting on the word of *Allah*. This even applies to those engaged in *Sufism*, or Islamic mysticism.

Chapter 4

Secular and Holy

Not only is action a form of worship, but at the same time there is no such thing as a separation between secular and holy within the Islamic worldview. Islam is about everything, from the way one performs prostrations of prayer to the way one governs a state. Western views of religion are by and large not like this, though at one time they were. For example, prior to the Enlightenment period (around 1700) the Christian worldview was considered universal in much of Europe. This did not mean that everyone was a Christian believer, yet Christian concepts of law determined right and wrong in the public sector. Indeed, one could say there were two forms of salvation in the European Christian experience, one deeply personal which impacted the very thought and heart, and one which was superficial and focused only on external factors such as obedience to the laws of the state.

Thus, one could not be a Christian in the first sense, but could have been part of a culture that was under Christian morality and law. This latter concept can in many ways explain many of the various crusades that were launched against non-Christian neighbors, such as The Holy Roman Empire's campaigns against the Saxons in the 9th century or against the Livonians in the 12th, or French campaigns against the Albigensians in the 13th. In many cases, the crusading operations were launched to compel a neighbor to submit to Christian authority and law, or at least a form as understood by the Catholic Church at that time.

I am not suggesting here that these Crusades are either good or bad; rather, I'm pointing out that at one time Europe considered Christianity important enough to be the basis of public law and order. And as a basis for law and order, those who did not hold to the same form could find themselves classified as outlaws. As a footnote, it should be stated that before some readers become too hasty in condemning crusading Christians they should consider the sins of those who engaged in similar campaigns in the name of other religions, or even in the name of secularism.

But while religion was a vital factor in daily public life in medieval Europe, much of this changed after the 1700s. Due to a series of disasters, among them the Thirty Years War (1618-1648), European Christianity began a retreat into a personal religion often called pietism. Christians began to separate their lives between the holy and the secular, where the former began to have next to no impact on the latter. In this new vision, what really mattered to the Christian involved church worship, prayer, and studying the Bible. This process of separation began to infiltrate into the United States in the mid-1700s and accelerated after the bloodletting of the American Civil War in the 1860s. American Christians may have found that singing the rousing tune of the "Battle Hymn of the Republic" could be inspiring in church, but more and more lost their desire to engage in religious crusades in the public square.

This tendency to separatism in Christianity between secular and holy spheres has some inadvertent support from the Bible itself, in large measure because of its somewhat artificial division between an Old and New Testament. The Old Testament was seen as the source of a judgmental God of vengeance, basing His wrath on the law, while the New Testament was seen as the source of a God of love and forgiveness, a reprieve from the harsh conception of God promoted in the ancient world. This Gnostic conception of God ("I believe in the loving God of the New Testament, and not the vengeful God of wrath of the Old Testament," a phrase very popular with some today) helped to create this separation of secular from holy, though it is actually not well supported by the Biblical documents. As a consequence, the sphere of religion became the domain of the family, women, and the church, while the secular domain became the realm of such things as men, politics and business.

In contrast, the Islamic worldview has little in it to suggest a separation between the secular and holy spheres. Indeed, if anything it is quite the opposite. In the early days of Islam there was more of a tendency of Muhammad and his followers to stay aloof from the political world. But this changed as the Islamic movement grew in strength and stature, until its worldview consumed all aspects of life. Therefore, the authentic fully developed Islamic worldview is not a retreat of religion into one's personal life, shunning the world around it, but rather is a full-scale onslaught into the public sphere. It is for this reason that Islam bears the name that it does: submission. It is not just the submission of your heart intentions to *Allah*, but the submission of your entire body and life to *Allah*'s will, and thus the essence of one's contract with *Allah*. In this manner Islam reflects the absolutism of the old Christianity in Europe, where everything was joined under the lordship of Jesus Christ and the church. To not understand this is once again to template modern Western notions of religion on Islam. The Islamic worldview does not separate its worldview into multiple spheres, with areas untouched by *shari`ah*.

Chapter 5

The Scales of Good and Evil

Unlike the Judeo-Christian worldview, there is no propitiation for sin in Islam. When one hears about Muslims sacrificing animals during the *hajj*, or pilgrimage to *Makkah*, such sacrifices are not atonement for sin. Instead, they are offered up to acknowledge the lordship of *Allah*, and then the meat is eaten and shared with the poor who cannot afford to make such sacrifices. In the Judeo-Christian worldview, there is a concept by which God receives a sacrifice in lieu of the penalty that should be meted out to the one separated from God by sin.

In Islam, there is no notion of being joined to *Allah* in the way that Christianity speaks of being joined to Christ, for in Islam *Allah* is so utterly different from mankind that there can never be any kind of direct fellowship.[10] *Allah* is totally transcendent, completely separated from mankind not

---

[10] For an example of this, see Ibn Ata *Allah* al-Iskandari. *Miftah al-Falah wa Misbah al-Arwah,* p. 113.

just because of man's sin, but by the simple fact that man is man and *Allah* is god. A Muslim can offer repentance and receive mercy from *Allah*, and indeed such mercy is absolutely essential to enter *jannah*, or paradise. But unlike grace in the Judeo-Christian worldview, mercy in Islam is essentially earned through daily actions.

As there is no conception of propitiation of sin, how does Islam view good and evil and how does one enter *jannah*? In the Islamic worldview good and evil essentially rest on a set of scales. While not often explicitly explained in this fashion in the early documents, the concept is present in the *hadith* literature and is later explained in more detail by the famous 13th century jurist Ibn Taymiyyah.[11] But to understand the issue of scales in Islam, one must first understand the Islamic conception of *jannah* (heaven or paradise) and *jahannam* (gehenna or hellfire). The descriptions of both in the Qur'an and especially *hadith* literature, are quite graphic and compelling. In *jannah*, the Muslim man lives like the noble lord he only wished he could live like on earth. He has more than enough to eat and drink, including alcoholic

---

[11] Surah 2:81-82; Surah 21:94; *Jami` al-Tirmidhi*, Sec. 35, The Days of Judgment, #2418; Ibn Taymiyyah, *Kitab al-Iman*, pp 316-328, 347-352.

beverages, and has more sex than he knows what to do with. And while the Qur'an and *hadith* literature are by and large silent about what women will receive in *jannah*,[12] such discussions about this foible miss the point about the purpose of *jannah*: that paradise is at minimum the place for Muslim men who have sacrificed much in this life to have abundance in the hereafter. Compared to *jannah*, *jahannam*, or the hellfire, is described in much more lurid detail and is quite gruesome. It is a fearsome place that one would wish to avoid with all their might.

And this brings us to our problem of scales of good and evil in Islam. To enter *jannah*, or paradise, requires actions from the Muslim coupled with mercy from *Allah*, and not just having the status of being a Muslim by name.[13] As the Muslim lives out his life, his actions by and large will be good or evil. As he does evil deeds, and just as importantly fails to do good deeds, the scales tip more against him and are a subtle reminder that he could very well spend time in the hellfire. In order to tip the scales back in his favor, he not only avoids evil deeds but also does good deeds, such as engaging in prayer and fasting, paying

---

[12] However, see *Tafsir Ibn Kathir*, Vol. 9, p. 400.

[13] Jamaal al-Din M. Zarabozo. *Purification of the Soul: Concept, Process and Means,* pp 195-198.

the *zakat* annual tax, or giving to the poor and visiting the sick. Doing such things tip the scales more towards *jannah*. For that matter, good deeds are ranked as to their importance in receiving virtue attained by them, with engaging in *jihad* or providing the logistical support for the same one of the highest.[14]

While good deeds can counterbalance evil, the problem faced by Muslims is that they really cannot know if they've ever done enough good deeds to gain that 51% necessary to overcome any evil or neglect of good from the past. Because of this, a Muslim is always in doubt about their future state in the afterlife.[15] If there is more weight on the wrong side of the scales, a Muslim will spend some time in the hellfire before being released to *jannah*. Considering the lurid descriptions of the hellfire, this is not a palatable prospect. Because of the doubt about his future state, a Muslim has basically two choices. He can continue to live day-to-day and hope that perhaps he will not spend any time in the hellfire. Or, he can do a very specific thing that can guarantee that he will never feel the flames of hell. That specific thing is a

---

[14] *Kitab al-Iman*, p. 23; *Purification of the Soul*, pp 201, 350-351.
[15] *Kitab al-Iman*, pp 402-404.

jihadi act that leads to martyrdom. Regarding the first, a Muslim can choose to wait and endure what may come, at least confident in the knowledge that one day, after his evil has been burned away, he will be released to *jannah*.[16]

In this context, the Islamic worldview in part resembles the Roman Catholic doctrine of purgatory. Those Muslims who have scales that are weighted more to the side of evil will get a chance to have their evil cleansed through fire and intercession of the angels. However, there is one group, specifically Christians that will never be allowed to escape the flames of hell, Christians because they believe in a concept called the Trinity. Thus, Christians are guilty of the "great wrongdoing" in Islam, called *shirk* or polytheism, and will thus spend eternity in *jahannam*.[17]

It is crucial to understand this notion of scales in Islam to understand the conduct of many individuals who engage in *jihadi* martyrdom acts. For while the typical Muslim may have to endure the

---

[16] For details regarding judgment scales in Islam, see *Tafsir Ibn Kathir*, Vol. 2, pp 52-53, 272-273, 434-435; Vol. 5, pp 123-124; Vol. 6, pp 296-298, 395, 694; Vol. 7, p. 159. Also see Surah 3:135.

[17] *Tafsir Ibn Kathir*, Vol. 7, p. 396.

hellfire for a limited period of time, there is one group that can completely avoid such consequences, specifically those who die, or intend to die, engaged in a *jihadi* act.[18] A *jihadi* act is when a Muslim decides that some kind of physical violence is necessary to assist in the imposition of Islam and the creation of a state ruled by *shari`ah*, or to avenge real or perceived insults of the Prophet Muhammad. Engaging in such a *jihadi* act, especially dying in the process is sufficient to usher the practitioner directly into *jannah*. In light of this, the actions of some jihadists in the past, actions that are often stated to be contrary to Islam can be understood. If engaging in *jihad* and becoming a *shahhid*, or martyr, releases the Muslim from the grips of *jahannam*, then it is understandable why Muslims with criminal or immoral backgrounds are susceptible to becoming *jihadists*, or why some who committed *jihadi* acts were seen days prior involved in what Westerners would consider acts not befitting what they think of a good Muslim. This latter point again demonstrates that far too many Western analysts continue to

---

[18] Surah 3:157; *Sahih al-Bukhari*, Vol. IV, #46, #66; *al-Muwatta of Imam Malik,* 21.15.35; *Sunan Abu Dawud*, Vol. II, Bk VIII, Chap. 858 #2489; *Jami` at-Tirmidhi*, Vol. 3, Sec. 20, Chap 4 #1632, #1640, #1653. *Tafsir Ibn Kathir*, Vol. 2, p. 302; Ahmad ibn Naqib al-Misri, *`Umdat al-Salik*, q2.4(4).

template Western religious notions of morality on Islam.

Regarding the issue of *jihadi* acts, the item that comes readily to most minds is the Islamic suicide bomber. Naturally, some may point out that suicide is wrong in Islam and thus cannot be used during something like a *jihadi* act. While suicide is indeed forbidden in Islam, it is defined as ending one's life without purpose.[19] In contrast, there is *hadith* literature support for surrendering one's life during *jihadi* acts in the midst of battle, and it is clear that engaging in such actions is not considered suicide by legal definition in Islam.[20] It is for this reason that so-called "suicide bombing" has not only received endorsement by some Islamic jurists, but even has a strong appeal to the rank and file in the Muslim community.[21]

---

[19] *Sahih al-Bukari*, Vol. II, #445, Vol. VII, #670; *Jami` at-Tirmidhi*, Vol. 3, Sec. 20, Chap 4 #1659; *Tafsir Ibn Kathir*, Vol. 2, pp 432-434.

[20] *Tafsir Ibn Kathir*, Vol. 1, p. 538; There are examples during Muhammad's lifetime that such immediate access to paradise was offered to those willing to die during a given battle. For a more complete analysis see my essay "Purifying the Heart: Suicide... or Jihadi Acts?" in *Terrorism's Unanswered Questions*, pp 129-141.

[21] "Islamic Extremism: Common Concern for Muslim and Western Publics," Pew Research Center, 2005, p 2; "Muslim

Many who practice a form of folk Islam will not understand the concept of the scales, and even those who are serious about Islamic practice often miss it.[22] Yet, those who move out of folk Islam to authentic Islam will often discover the idea, either because of what they have been taught or simply from studying the early Islamic sources. It is through such a "revival" process, where an errant Muslim or new convert is exposed to the early sources of Islam, that one finds the road to what is often called "radicalization." Many who speak of radicalization rarely if ever define the source of such radicalizing. If they do, they typically blame the aforementioned jurist Ibn Taymiyyah or the Wahhabis, a group of Muslims in Arabia in the 1700s who were experiencing a revival of early Islamic practice. I have rarely seen any analyst explain that the root of this so-called "radicalization" is from the initial sources of Islam and the life of the Prophet Muhammad.

Americans: Middle Class and Mostly Mainstream," Pew Research Center, 2007, p. 32; "Muslim Publics Divided on Hamas and Hezbollah," Pew Research Center, 2010, p. 18.
[22] While I was providing a training session for American personnel in Saudi Arabia, I had a Muslim challenge me, saying "where do you get this stuff?"

What makes this issue of scales between good and evil so crucial? If a Muslim has been negligent of his Islamic duties, or even worse has also been involved in egregious evil (as defined by Islam), then a revival of Islam can easily provide the impetus for him to throw himself into a *jihadi* act, even one that involves a suicide mission. I do not assert this lightly, for we have already seen numerous examples of those who have done such *jihadi* acts who have had very checkered pasts, both by Western and Islamic standards.

However, having said this I must issue a word of caution. Some may come to the conclusion that the solution to putting an end to *jihadi* acts is to see a revival of Islam where a Muslim adheres more closely to the *shari`ah*. This is fallacious because in Islam *jihad* is a required duty regardless of one's own moral standing. Either one should directly engage in *jihad* or support others in *jihad* with finances, protection, and encouragement.[23] *Jihad* as a military action is a normative command in Islam. Unlike the

---

[23] Surah 61:2-4; *Sunan Abu Dawud*, Vol. II, Bk VIII, Chap. 865 #2496; *Sahih al-Bukhari*, Vol. I, #25; Vol. IV, #41, #92; Vol. V, #598, #600. Regarding support, see *Sunan Ibn-e-Majah*, #2758, #2759; Sahih al-Bukhari, Vol. IV, #94; *Jami` at-Tirmidhi*, Vol. 3, Sec. 20, Chap 4 #1625, #1626, #1628, #1636; *al-Muqaddimah*, Vol. 1, p. 473.

one-time command of Jehovah to the Israelites to march into Canaan and kill the inhabitants, the command in Islam to fight for the sake of *Allah* and *Allah*'s prophet Muhammad is without restriction to place or time. Therefore, there is always an affirmative command for a Muslim to engage in some type of warfare, and this warfare need not be in groups or under the leadership of any government. Indeed, within the Hanafi *madhhab*, which encompasses the largest body of Islamic believers, the leader of an Islamic state is to give after the fact endorsement to *jihadi* raids waged by individuals, even if they did so without his knowledge or permission.[24]

---

[24] *Al-Hidayah*, Book XIII, Chap 111.1.

Chapter 6

Three Stages in Islam

One aspect of Islam that is relatively unknown to many Western people is the concept of stages within Islamic practice. Oftentimes, Westerners are bombarded with Islamic quotations in the media, whether from the Qur'an or *hadith* literature, that contradicts the notion of *jihad*, which is the use of violence to impose submission to *shari`ah* or as a means to avenge insult to the Prophet Muhammad. Such quotes naturally raise the question, how can some Muslims be so violent if the Qur'an is so focused on peacefulness? The answer to this lies in the nature of the Qur'an and when passages were recited.

During the lifetime of the Prophet Muhammad, there were basically two places where Qur'anic passages were initially recited, first *Makkah* and then *Madinah*. And while there is some measure of doubt as to where some passages were recited, there's enough evidence in most cases to pinpoint where passages were recited and in what context that helps to determine the character of what was said and meant.

When Muhammad first publically declared that he was the Prophet of *Allah*, his followers amounted to only a few people in his immediate family. After a few years of preaching, his following was so small as to amount to less than one percent of the population of *Makkah*. During this time, his preaching was exclusively devoted to peaceful coexistence and tolerance. Thus, the passages in the Qur'an that advocate accepting other worldviews and religious ideas alongside Islam come from his early years in *Makkah*. This period amounts to what can be referred to as Stage 1 Islam. This stage was about tolerance because the Islamic movement was so small that any call to exclusivity or fighting could lead to it being crushed with ease.

Just prior to his migration to *Madinah*, Muhammad converted some powerful individuals, both physically and economically. At this point, the recitations began to change in quality, with a turn towards self-defense as a motif for the Islamic community. Thus, with a little more physical power backing him up, Muhammad was able to ward off any violence from opponents of Islam in *Makkah*, even engaging in some counter-violence of his own. This period is what can be called Stage 2 Islam. During this period, there is in essence a form of cold war between Islam and competing worldviews and can be summed up as a period devoted to self-defense from attacks and persecution.

Once Muhammad and many of his followers left *Makkah* for *Madinah*, they were still in the self-defense mode of Stage 2. However, this lasted only about nine months, and then shifted to an offensive posture. At this point, recitations take on a much more absolutist and aggressive tone, and offensive operations against Muhammad's enemies soon followed. This period constitutes Stage 3 Islam, a period of offensive warfare waged against those who refuse to submit to Islamic governance and decrees. There is no longer any language about tolerance and acceptance of other worldviews. There is Islam and Islam only, culminating in the conquest of *Makkah* in AD 630 and the destruction of the hundreds of idols in the *Ka`bah*, the cube-shaped structure that serves as both the center of *Makkah* and the world.[25]

---

[25] The destruction of these idols and any legal concepts attached to them demonstrated that in Stage 3 of Islam there is no longer any notion of tolerance for "the other."

This understanding of Stages in Islam are known and emulated by Islamic groups throughout history.[26] As such, there are no set time frames between stages, but the pattern of tolerance to self-defense to offensive warfare is quite clear. It is through these stages that Muhammad practiced Islam, for while Islam is indeed personal it is also very political, and as such it engages in actions as any other political entity would pursue. Islamic movements in other places and times have followed this pattern with consistent regularity.

Initial settlements develop in a foreign land, often spearheaded by merchants who move about freely and are able to report to Islamic authorities about an area's strengths and weaknesses. During this time, the settlement calls for tolerance in an effort to maintain its foothold, even as other Islamic groups engage in a series of raids into the enemy territory. Once the settlement becomes strong enough it develops a policy of active defense, and further strengthening brings it to the offensive stage where its actions are merged with the various raiding groups.

---

[26] Examples can be found in *Tafsir Ibn Kathir*, Vol. 2, p. 233; Ibn Taymiyyah, *On Public and Private Law,* p. 135; Sayyid Qutb, *Milestones*, p. 64; Abdullahi Ahmed an-Na'im, *Toward an Islamic Reformation,* pp 145-147, 158-159.

Indeed, this methodology was not new with Muhammad, and would be used by many other cultures as a classical form of insurgency.[27]

---

[27] For examples see, *al-Muqaddimah*, Vol. 2, pp 128-135; Widukind of Corvey, *The Three Books of the Deeds of the Saxons*, pp 162-167; Henricus Lettus, *The Chronicle of Henry of Livonia;* Thomas Walker Arnold, *The Preaching of Islam: A History of the Propagation of the Muslim Faith,* pp 251-257.

Chapter 7

Taqlid and *Ijtihad*

How does a Muslim come to know the things I have discussed so far? Essentially, there are two methods a Muslim can use, *taqlid* or *ijtihad*. Often loosely though somewhat incorrectly rendered as "blind following," *taqlid* is the process by which a Muslim learns the doctrines of Islam from a teacher. In contrast, *ijtihad* is the method in which a Muslim works through the Islamic texts on their own to determine what they say.[28]

The process of *taqlid* is pretty much what most people do in all cultures on a day-to-day basis. None of us can know everything, so we come to rely upon a group of competent people or experts to provide us needed information on various issues. From fixing a car's engine to flying an airplane, or from performing brain surgery or planting a garden, all of us turn to a subject matter expert to give us

---

[28] For an excellent overview of *ijtihad* and *taqlid*, see Imran Ahsan Khan Nyazee, *The Methodology of Ijtihad.*

insight on how to do these things, or to do them for us. This is a reality of life, and certainly throws out the entire premise of the Enlightenment Project where Immanuel Kant tells us that we should shed all notions of relying on others for facts and information.[29] Kant's real target in stressing this was the Bible and Christian authorities such as the church (whether Catholic or Protestant). Even Kant understood that nobody could know everything, but wanted to see Christianity expunged from public life. In Islam, the process of *taqlid* is where Muslims, busy with day-to-day life, rely upon *imams*, or clergy, to teach them how to do what Islam demands.

On the other hand, *ijtihad* is opposite of *taqlid* in the sense that it calls upon the Muslim to study the early Islamic texts for themselves. The root word is the same from which is derived the word *jihad*, and essentially means that a Muslim "struggles" with the texts to determine what they are saying to him in his current life context. For a number of centuries, it had been the basic teaching of Islam that *ijtihad* no longer

---

[29] Kant, "Was ist Aufklärung." In this essay, Kant informs his readers that to gain true enlightenment one must leave a self-imposed nonage of reliance on authorities to become the final decision maker on all things that affect their life.

applied, and that a Muslim should simply follow the lead of their *imams* and scholars.

And this brings me to the assertion of some in the West that the Islamic world could moderate, moving away from violent *jihad* and its absolutist premises if only individual Muslims would experience the revival of *ijtihad*. On the surface this sounds so good. After all, wouldn't it be better if individual Muslims learned of Islam for themselves instead of being pushed along by the whims and wishes of *imams*? But therein lies the most egregious of errors.

While *ijtihad* does indeed call upon a Muslim to learn of Islam on his own, it doesn't give him the liberty to interpret it as he wills. While it does allow for Islam to develop ways to apply the *shari`ah* to new situations, it doesn't mean that the foundational concepts become defunct. Put another way, the fundamentals of Islam are already carved in stone, and no process of *ijtihad* can alter this.[30] The principle that the sayings and deeds of Muhammad are the basis of the Muslim's life will not change, and within that body of teaching is the need to engage in

---

[30] An-Na'im, *Toward an Islamic Reformation,* pp 27-29; Souad T. Ali, *A Religion, Not a State: Ali `Abd al-Raziq's Islamic Justification of Political Secularism,* pp 57-58.

or support *jihad* to impose Islam on others. This cannot and will not change unless a Muslim jettisons the principles of Muhammad's teachings, and once they do that they are no longer practicing authentic Islam but a form of folk Islam.

It is of course possible that a Muslim, practicing *ijtihad*, could decide that certain commands of Islam no longer apply to him and enter that realm of folk religion. However, it is just as possible, and even more so, that he will instead discover commands that his *imams* have been disinclined to promote. The advantage of *taqlid* for the West is that such *imams*, more concerned about a forceful reaction by governments that could cause them to lose their positions and status, will steer their followers away from things like violent *jihad* and into other more peaceful pursuits.[31] A revival of *ijtihad* would break down the authority of many *imams*, allowing individual Muslims to discover doctrines within Islam that have been largely kept from them, including some I have discussed in this book. Instead of mitigating violence, it will actually encourage it, creating a whole host of lone wolf actors bent on

---

[31] Emmanuel Sivan, *Radical Islam: Medieval Theology and Modern Politics*, pp 54, 55.

purifying their hearts through a *jihadi* act. And in this sense, a revival of *ijtihad* is another part in the process of so-called "radicalization."

Chapter 8

The Muslim and the West

I now turn to examine the authentic Muslim's view of the Western world. In a nutshell, Muslims love Western technology, and indeed cannot get enough of it. However, they disdain and reject Western philosophy, whether it is secular Enlightenment era thought or Western Christianity. Therefore, Westerners are often treated to statements by Islamic writers attempting to highlight how much they love the Western world. However, a close examination of such writings shows that what they really love is Western technology.

Many do not realize how important this issue is. The modern technology of the West is an extension of the West's worldview, and not just some random happenstance. Islamic writers by and large do not make this connection, believing instead that their own culture was somehow cheated of having all this nice stuff and a great future.[32] While there are some examples of medieval Islam making contributions to science and learning, by and large they copied science from the Western world, whether it be Greek philosophy or scientific laws discovered by Christians. One author asserts that Islam has not discovered one basic scientific law, or any of the great discoveries in physics, chemistry, electricity, or medicine.[33]

The realm of philosophy is the realm of morals. And while I would take umbrage with some aspects of Western morals, Islam takes offense at the entire body of Western morals, whether secular or Christian. Moreover, the Islamic worldview does not intersect with Western conceptions of government such as democracy and the rule of law. This rejection of law and culture is reflected in the development of Islamic communities in the Western world, where Muslims tend to self-ghettoize or cocoon thereby developing exclusive enclaves.[34] Following the three

---

[32] The entire thrust of Tamim Ansary's book *Destiny Disrupted* is that the West cheated the Islamic world.

[33] Alvin J. Schmidt, *The Great Divide: The Failure of Islam and the Triumph of the West,* pp 200-201.

[34] Discussions regarding such cocooning can be found in Melanie Phillips, *Londonistan,* and Abigail R. Esman, *Radical State: How Jihad is Winning Over Democracy in the West.* For a Muslim view, though dated, of this phenomenon see *Muslim*

stages of Islam explained earlier, these enclaves will continue to grow, fueled by both immigration and a very high birthrate. Such demographic warfare will ultimately consume a host culture that refuses to have children. Europe is just beginning to understand this, but far too late.

Because authentic Islam cannot accept other philosophical worldviews, it cannot ultimately reform or change so long as the early Islamic documents form the basis of the religion. There can be revival in Islam, but not reform. Thus, a culture that has a form of folk Islam as its religious base can have a revival of authentic Islam, because the revival is based on a call to return to the early writings and ideas of the Qur'an and *hadith* literature. This process has been seen in our day in what has been euphemistically labeled the "Arab Spring." In reality, this movement is more like the "Islamic Spring," as a revival of authentic Islam sweeping across the Middle East and North Africa.[35] Concurrently, a culture can "reform"

Communities in Non-Muslim States, a collection of papers from a conference held by the Islamic Council of Europe in July 1978.
[35] For a review of the background to this awakening, see Martin Kramer, *Arab Awakening & Islamic Revival;* Carrie Rosefsky Wickham, *Mobilizing Islam: Religion, Activism, and Political Change in Egypt;* Quintan Wiktorowicz, *Islamic Activism: A Social Movement Theory Approach;* Eleanor Abdella Doumato and Gregory Starrett, eds., *Teaching Islam: Textbooks and*

from authentic Islam into a type of folk Islam. This has been seen by and large in the Middle Eastern world from the late medieval period into the modern age (AD 1500-1900).

Religion in the Middle East. For a Muslim view, see Yusuf al-Qaradawi, *Priorities of the Islamic Movement in the Coming Phase,* and *Islamic Awakening: Between Rejection & Extremism.*

Conclusion

Far too often, Western analysts attempt to template Western notions of morality and reason on Islam. This is a serious error, an error that will lead to incorrect conclusions and thus often fueling the skewed perception of Islam we see in popular Western media. By failing to understand the worldview of the authentic Muslim, and the sources of that worldview, analysts create a false impression of the movement, and this false impression has a serious impact on popular understanding as well. The purpose of this little book has been to examine the essential yet not so obvious points regarding the authentic Islamic worldview.

I have examined the concept regarding practice and doing the right things as the key process for the Muslim to reach *jannah*. Also discussed were the notions that a Muslim must not separate his spiritual from his secular life, and that he must be careful of what he does and does not do lest the scales of judgment tip against him, sending him to spend a period of time in the hellfire. I also explained how Islam migrates itself to non-Muslim lands, using a series of stages that are actually quite common to all insurgency movements. I then delved into the processes of *taqlid* and *ijtihad*, demonstrating that a revival of *ijtihad* is no panacea for the violence many in the world have experienced from Islamic *jihadi* acts. Finally, I have delved briefly into the Islamic rejection of Western ideas even as they soak up Western technology, and how this has led to self-ghettoizing by Islamic groups in the West.

What can be seen from looking at these few issues regarding an authentic Muslim's worldview is the incredible challenge he has in trying to maintain some kind of lifestyle that may seem ordinary to the typical Westerner. With the constant threat of hellfire tugging at his elbow, and the need to constantly be engaged in various acts that would be considered pleasing to *Allah*, such as the five daily prayers and other restrictions on behavior, one can sense that he would feel his life is very different and unique. This could be either a bad or good thing. In one way, he may feel totally overwhelmed by the demands of a god who is far removed from human existence and needs, and yet he may believe that he is indeed something special, a select elite chosen by *Allah* as a special servant.

In either case, the demands and expectations on his entire life could be enough to push him beyond the norm of daily life. On the one hand he can be pitied, because of the frustration he would feel in laboring under such a yoke. And on the other hand he should be feared, because those around him may never quite know what he ultimately will do. In this regard, and with the earliest Islamic sources opposed to reform, the threat of ongoing conflict with elements of the Islamic world is both real and pervasive.

Glossary of Terms

I use Arabic terms where appropriate in places, but not their plural versions so as to avoid confusion for those who are not specialists in Arabic. I have done this because these terms do not lend themselves to easy translation, and secondly to familiarize readers with them.

Allah- Arabic term for the one god of Islam. While often rendered as "God" in English, it is considered a proper noun and should not be translated.

Din- A contract in which one is indebted to another. Rendered in English as "religion" in most works.

Fiqh- the process of Islamic jurisprudence conducted by Islamic *qadis*, or judges.

Hadith- the sayings of Muhammad other than the Qur'an, often mixed with the *sunnah*.

Hafiz- one who memorizes the Qur'an. Those who memorize most of the *hadith* literature also have this honorific.

Hajj- the annual pilgrimage to *Makkah*, as one of the five pillars of Islam.

Ijtihad- in contrast to *taqlid*, the process by which a Muslim searches Islamic texts to gain his own understanding rather than merely accepting another's viewpoint.

Imam- a clergy member in Islam.

Iman- faith or trust that one has in *Allah*.

Jahannam (hell)- the hellfire, a terrible place in Islam for those who are disobedient to *Allah*.

Jannah (heaven; paradise)- the beautiful destination for Muslims

Jihad- while there are other concepts of *jihad*, or struggle, it is used here to denote a physical or military struggle to impose *shari`ah*.

Ka`bah- the cube shaped structure in *Makkah* that is considered the center of the world in Islam.

Madhhab- an Islamic school of law.

Madinah (Medina)- the City of the Prophet Muhammad, where he migrated to after leaving *Makkah*. Formerly known as Yathrib.

Makkah (Mecca)- the city where the Ka`bah is located. It is considered holy in Islam and no non-Muslim is allowed to enter.

Qadi- a judge regarding the application of Islamic law.

Salafi- the earliest companions of the Prophet Muhammad, and those to be most emulated.

Shahhid- a martyr who is killed for Islam.

**Shari`ah**- the Islamic law. The purpose of *jihad* is to impose *shari`ah* on all the earth.

Shirk- polytheism. Also applied to Christians who hold to the doctrine of the Trinity.

Sirah- the historical literature of early Islam. Often a mix of *hadith* and *sunnah*.

Sufism- Islamic mysticism. However, more mystical versions are considered heretical by many Muslim leaders.

Sunnah- the acts of Muhammad, often mixed with the *hadith*.

Surah- a chapter within the Qur'an.

Taqlid- often rendered as "blind following" and contrasted to *ijtihad*, it is the idea that a Muslim submits himself to the teachings of an imam or scholar rather than searching out details for himself.

Tafsir- a commentary on the Qur'an that explains the historical and philosophical context.

Zakat- the annual tax on Muslims that amounts to 2 ½% of accumulated wealth.

Works Cited

Hadith Collections:

Al-Muwatta of Imam Malik ibn Anas. Translated by Aisha Abdarrahman Bewley. Inverness, Scotland: Madinah Press, 2004.

Jami` at-Tirmidhi. Translated by Abu Khaliyl. Riyadh, Saudi Arabia: Darussalam, 2007.

Sahih al-Bukhari, Vols I-IX. Translated by Muhammad Muhsin Khan. New Delhi: Kitab Bhavan, 1987.

Sahih Imam Muslim. Vols. 1-8. Translated by Abdul Hamid Siddiqi. New Delhi: Idara Isha'at-E-Diniyat Ltd., 2001.

Sunan Abu Dawud. Vols I-III. Translated by Ahmad Hasan. New Delhi: Kitab Bhavan, 2005.

Sunan Ibn-e-Majah. Vols I-V. Translated by Muhammad Tufail Ansari. New Delhi: Kitab Bhavan, 2004.

Medieval Islamic Sources

*Al-Hidayah Fi Sharh Bidayat al-Mubtadi (*as *The Guidance)*. Vols I and II. Translated by Imran Ahsan Khan Nyazee. Bristol, England: Amal Press, 2008.

Al-Iskandari, Ibn Ata *Allah. Miftah al-Falah wa Misbah al-Arwah (*as *The Key to Salvation)*. Cambridge, UK: The Islamic Texts Society, 1996.

Al-Misri, Ahmad ibn Naqib. `*Umdat al-Salik (Reliance of the Traveller)*. Translated by Nuh Ha Mim Keller. Beltsville, Md.: Amana Publications, 1994.

Al-Tabari, Abu Ja'far Muhammad bin Jarir. *Kitab al-Jihad (The Book of Jihad)*. Translated by Yasir S. Ibrahim. Lewiston, N.Y.: Edwin Mellen Press, 2007.

Ibn al-Salah al-Shahrazuri, *Kitab Ma`rifat anwa` ilm al-hadith (*as *An Introduction to the Science of the Hadith*. Translated by Eerik Dickinson. Reading, UK: Garent Publishing Ltd., 2006.

Ibn Kathir, *Tafsir Ibn Kathir*. Shaykh Safiur-Rahman al-Mubarakpuri, ed. Riyadh, Saudi Arabia: Darussalam, 2003.

Ibn Khaldûn, *The Muqaddimah: An Introduction to History,* Vols. 1-3. Translated by Franz Rosenthal. Princeton, N.J.: Princeton University Press, 1980.

Ibn Taymiyyah. *Al-Siyasa al-shar`iyya fi islah al-ra`t wa al-ra`iyya (*as *Public and Private Law in Islam.*

Translated by Omar A. Farrukh. Beirut, Lebanon: Khayat Book & Publishing Co., 1966.

_____, *Kitab al-Iman (The Book of Faith)*.Translated by Salman Hassan al-Ani and Shadia Ahmad Tel. Bloomington, Ind.: Iman Publishing House, 1999.

Other Sources

Al-Hashimi, Muhammad Ali. *The Ideal Muslim Society.* Riyadh, Saudi Arabia: International Islamic Publishing House, 2007.

Ali, Souad T. *A Religion, Not a State: Ali `Abd al-Raziq's Islamic Justification of Political Secularism.* Salt Lake City: University of Utah Press, 2009.

Al-Qaradawi, Yusuf. *Priorities of the Islamic Movement in the Coming Phase.* Swansea,UK: Awakening Publications, 2000.
_____. *Islamic Awakening: Between Rejection & Extremism.* London: Zain International, 1991.

An-Na'im, Abdullahi Ahmed. *Toward an Islamic Reformation.* Syracuse, N.Y.: Syracuse University Press, 1990.

Ansary. Tamim. *Destiny Disrupted: A History of the World Through Islamic Eyes.* New York: Public Affairs, 2009.

Arnold, Thomas Walker. *The Preaching of Islam: A History of the Propagation of the Muslim Faith.* Westminster, UK: Archibald Constable & Co, 1896.

Doumato, Eleanor Abdella and Gregory Starrett, eds. *Teaching Islam: Textbooks and Religion in the Middle East.* Boulder, Colo.: Lynne Rienner Publishers, 2007.

Esman, Abigail R. *Radical State: How Jihad is Winning Over Democracy in the West.* Santa Barbara, Calf.: Praeger Security International, 2010.

Harris, Lee. *The Suicide of Reason: Radical Islam's Threat to the West.* New York: Basic Books, 2007.

Henricus Lettus, *The Chronicle of Henry of Livonia.* Translated by James A. Brundage. New York: Columbia University Press, 1961.

Hiebert, Paul G., and R. Daniel Shaw and Tite Tiénou. *Understanding Folk Religion.* Grand Rapids, MI: Baker Books, 1999.

Kant, Immanuel. "Was ist Aufklärung" (What is Enlightenment). Essay written in 1784.

Kramer, Martin. *Arab Awakening & Islamic Revival.* New Brunswick, N.J.: Transaction Publishers, 1996.

Lane, Edward W. *An Arabic-English Lexicon in Eight Parts.* Beirut, Lebanon: Librarie Du Liban, 1968.

Muslim Communities in Non-Muslim States. London: Islamic Council of Europe, 1980.

Nyazee, Imran Ahsan Khan. *The Methodology of Ijtihad.* Kuala Lumpur, Indonesia: Islamic Book Trust, 2002.

Pew Research Center. "Islamic Extremism: Common Concern for Muslim and Western Publics." 2005.

_____. "Muslim Americans: Middle Class and Mostly Mainstream." 2007.

_____. "Muslim Publics Divided on Hamas and Hezbollah." 2010.

Phillips, Melanie. *Londonistan.* New York: Encounter Books, 2006.

Qutb, Sayyid. *Milestones.* New Delhi: Islamic Book Service, 2005.

Reilly, Robert R. *The Closing of the Muslim Mind: How Intellectual Suicide Created the Modern Islamist Crisis.* Wilmington, Del.: ISI Books, 2010.

Rodgers, Russ. "Purifying the Heart: Suicide... or Jihadi Acts?" In *Terrorism's Unanswered Questions*, ed. Adam Lowther and Beverley Lindsay. Westport, Conn.: Praeger Security International, 2009.

Schmidt, Alvin J. *The Great Divide: The Failure of Islam and the Triumph of the West.* Boston: Regina Orthodox Press, 2004.

Sivan, Emmanuel. *Radical Islam: Medieval Theology and Modern Politics.* New Haven, Conn.: Yale University Press, 1990.

Wickham, Carrie Rosefsky. *Mobilizing Islam: Religion, Activism, and Political Change in Egypt.* New York: Columbia University Press, 2002.

Widukind of Corvey, *The Three Books of the Deeds of the Saxons.* Translated by Raymund F. Wood. Unpublished thesis, 1949.

Wiktorowicz, Quintan, ed. *Islamic Activism: A Social Movement Theory Approach.* Bloomington: University of Indiana Press, 2004.

Zarabozo, Jamaal al-Din M.. *Purification of the Soul: Concept, Process and Means.* Denver, Co.; al-Basheer Co., 2002.

For Further Reading

I have organized this in such a way that readers choose what works for them. While editions may vary, all of the below titles are in English.

For the beginner:

Glubb, Sir John. *The Life and Times of Muhammad.* New York: Cooper Square Press, 2001.

Moshay, G.J.O. *Who is This Allah?* Bucks, UK: Dorchester House Publications, 1995.

Samir, Samir Khalil, S.J. *111 Questions on Islam.* Translated by Father Wafik Nasry, S.J. San Francisco: Ignatius Press, 2008.

For the more advanced:

Ibn Ishaq. *Sirat Rasul Allah* (as *The Life of Muhammad*). Translated by A. Guillaume. Oxford, UK: Oxford University Press, 2004.

Haykal, Muhammad H. *The Life of Muhammad.* Translated by Ismai`il Raji al-Faruqi. Kuala Lumpur, Indonesia: Islamic Book Trust, 2002.

Al-Yahsubi, Qadi 'Iyad Ibn Musa. *Ash-Shifa (*as *Muhammad, Messenger of Allah).* Translated by Aisha Abdarrahman Bewley. Inverness, Scotland: Madinah Press, 2006.

Index

About the Author

Russ Rodgers is a military historian and former adjunct professor of history. A U.S. Army veteran with service in armor, infantry, and military intelligence, Rodgers is considered a subject matter expert on insurgency movements and early Islamic warfare. He is a sought after speaker and has lectured in such diverse venues as the Worldwide Anti-Terrorism Conference, the NATO School in Germany, and to military personnel in the United States as well as Kuwait and Saudi Arabia. He is the author of *The Generalship of Muhammad: Battles and Campaigns of the Prophet of Allah,* and *Fundamentals of Islamic Asymmetric Warfare: A Documentary Analysis of the Principles of Muhammad,* as well as numerous articles and essays.

To arrange to have Mr. Rodgers as a speaker for your church or civic organization, send your request to ritterorden2000@yahoo.com.

Made in the USA
San Bernardino, CA
10 February 2016